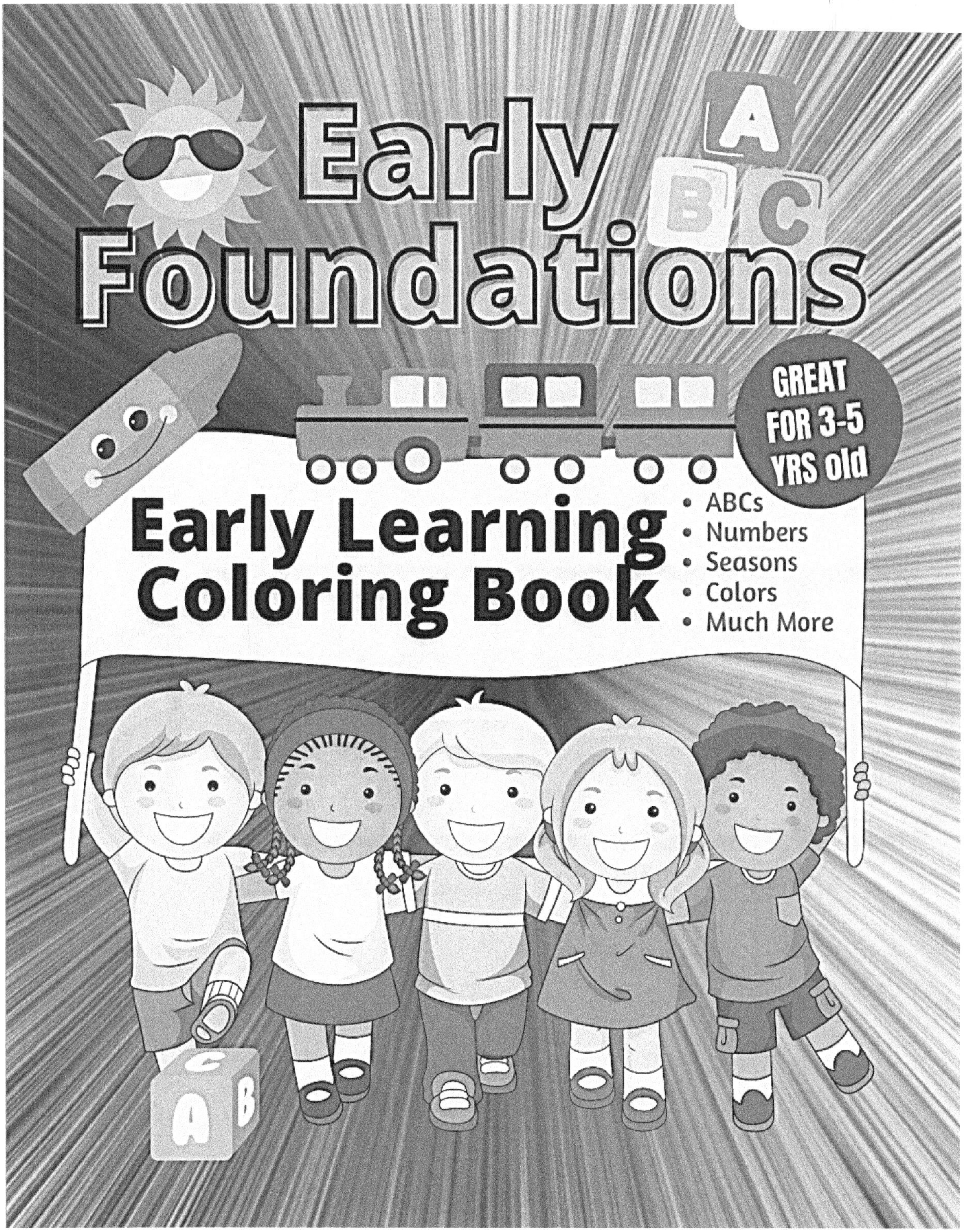
Early Foundations
A
B C
GREAT FOR 3-5 YRS old
Early Learning Coloring Book
• ABCs
• Numbers
• Seasons
• Colors
• Much More
C
A B

# This coloring book belongs to:

JahamaKidz  has carefully designed this "early learning coloring book" to introduce children ages 3 and up to a variety of concepts, such as:

Letters
Numbers
Colors
Shapes
Community helpers
Transportation
Much more.

Our goal is to help pre-K and kindergarten students to recognize letters, numbers, shapes, community helpers and all the other concept included in this coloring book; we also, look to reinforce their early learning in a fun and creative way, in this case by coloring, which is an activity that all children love and enjoy very much.



Contact Information:
Jahamapress@gmail.com

Cover designed by: Mariel Navarro
Interior design and content by: Mariel Navarro

Designed, developed and printed in the U.S.A.

ISBN: 9798583221981

# THE ALPHABET

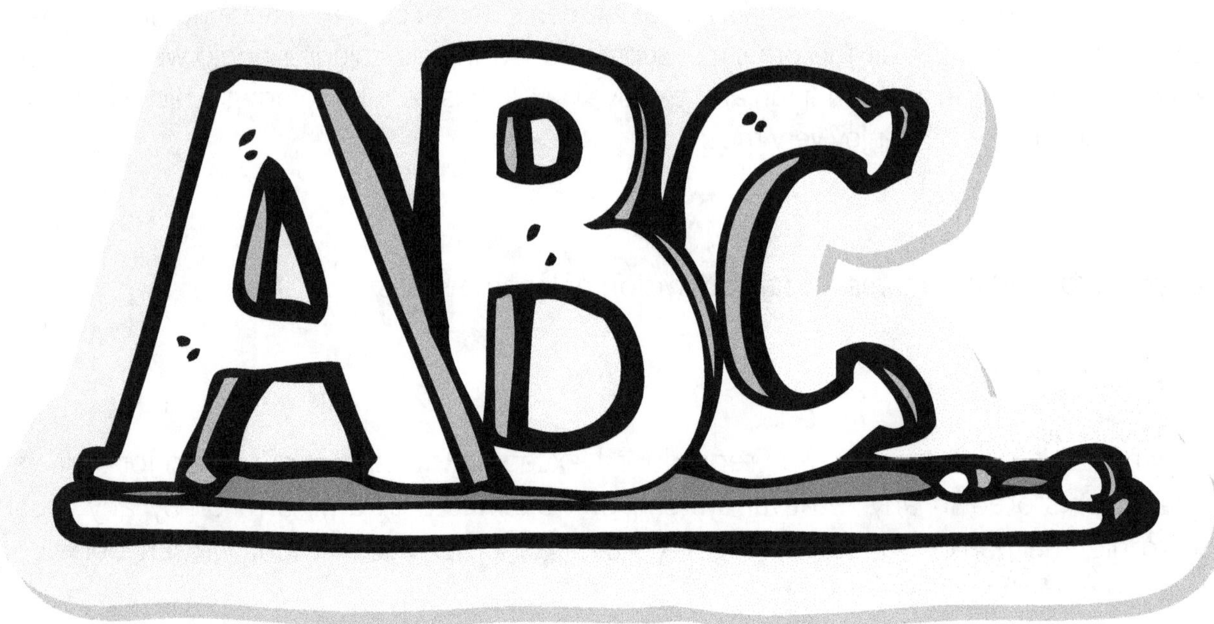

- Have the child color the animal, say the letter and the name of the animal out loud.
- Have them trace with a crayon or finger the inside of each letter that makes up the word, this could help them with their writing skills development.

Ant

Bear

Cow

# Dog

Elephant

Frog

# Giraffe

Hippo

Insect

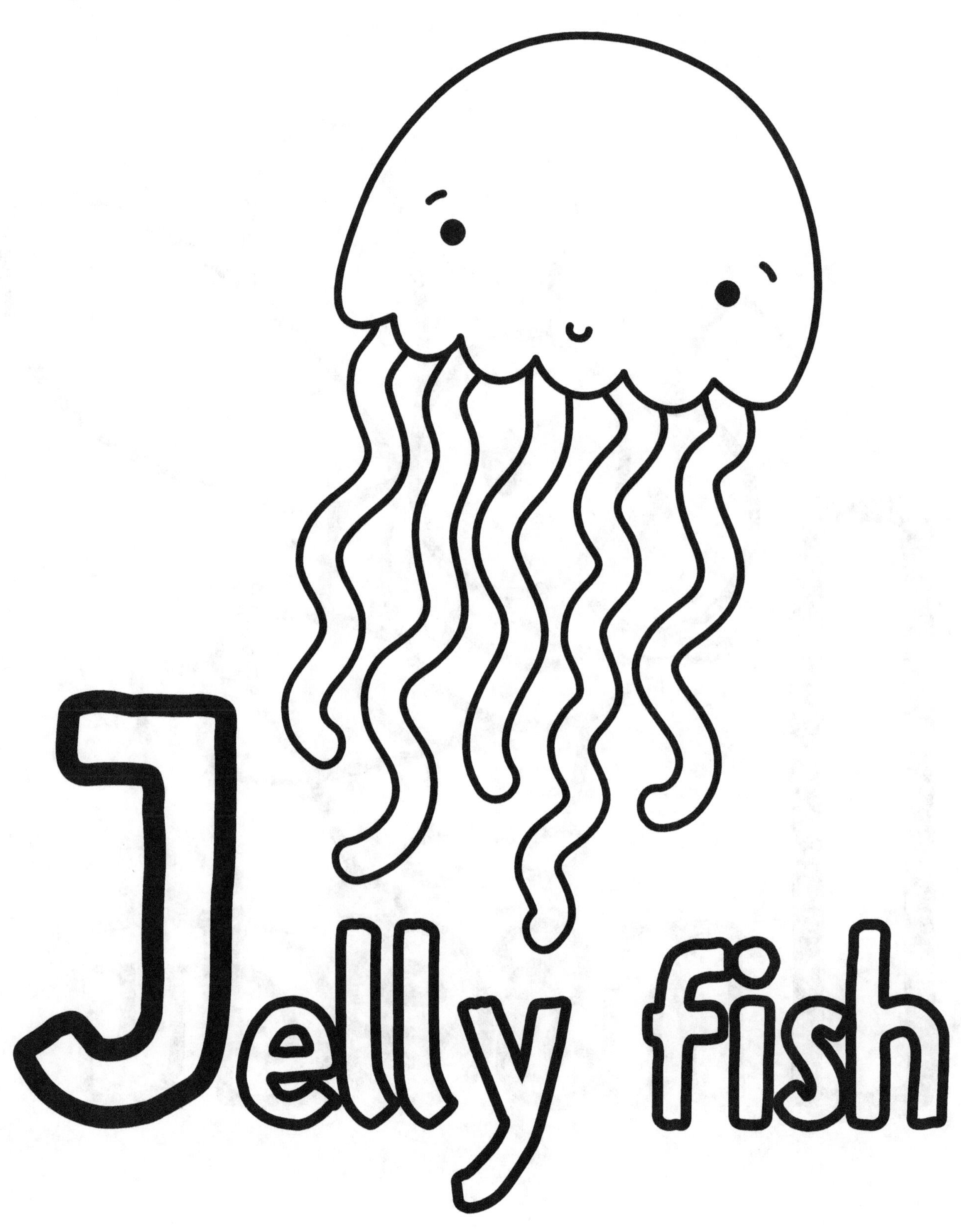

Jelly fish

Insect

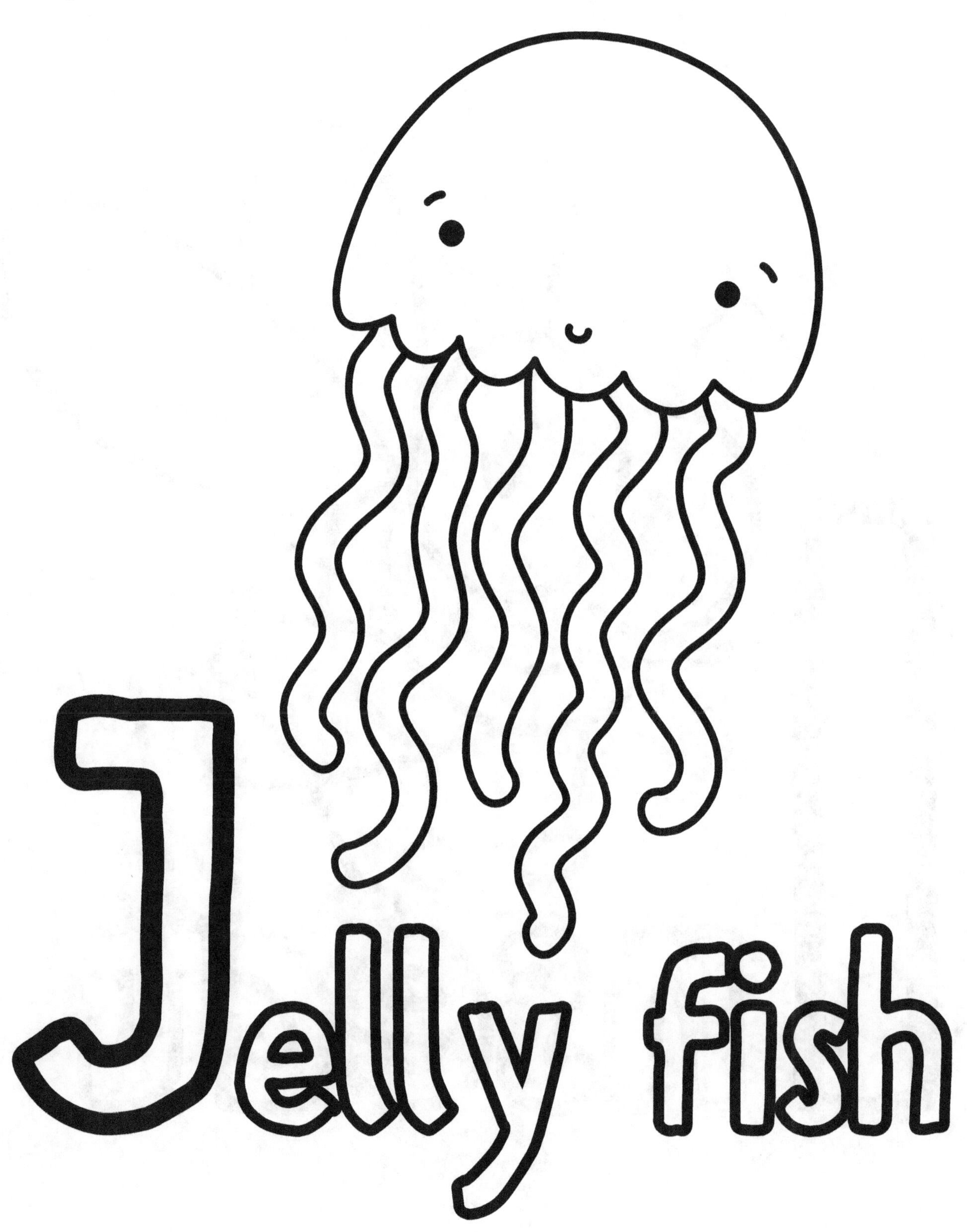


Jelly fish

Koala

Lion

# Monkey

Nest

Ostrish

Penguin

Quail

Rabbit

Shark

Turtle

Urial

Vole

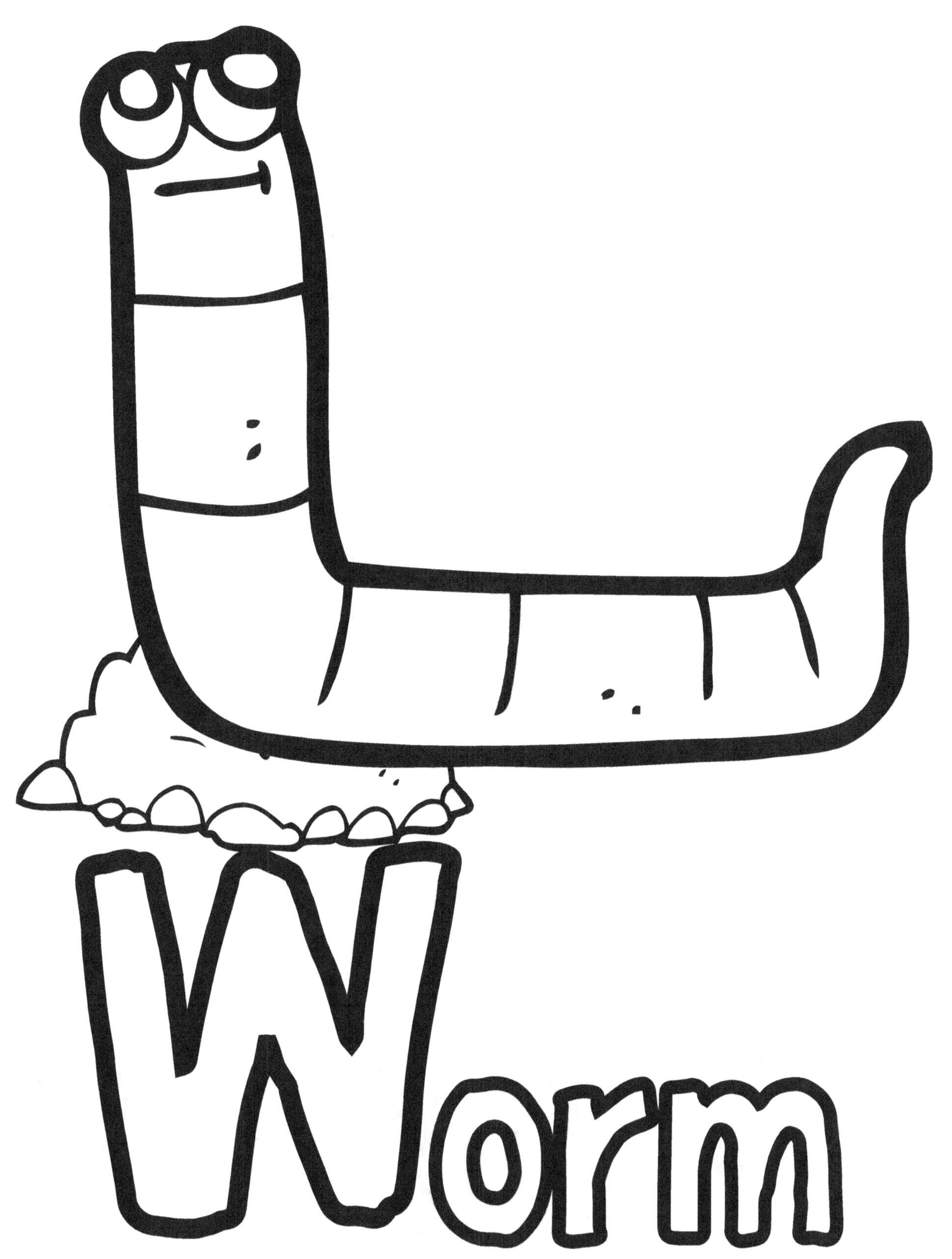
Worm

# X - ray fish

# Yak

# Zebra

# THE NUMBERS

# 123

- Have the child say the number as they color.
- Each number page has counters (circles) to help the child develop their counting skills. As they count, have them color in each counter.
- Besides coloring, have them trace inside each word with a crayon or finger as they say out loud each letter.

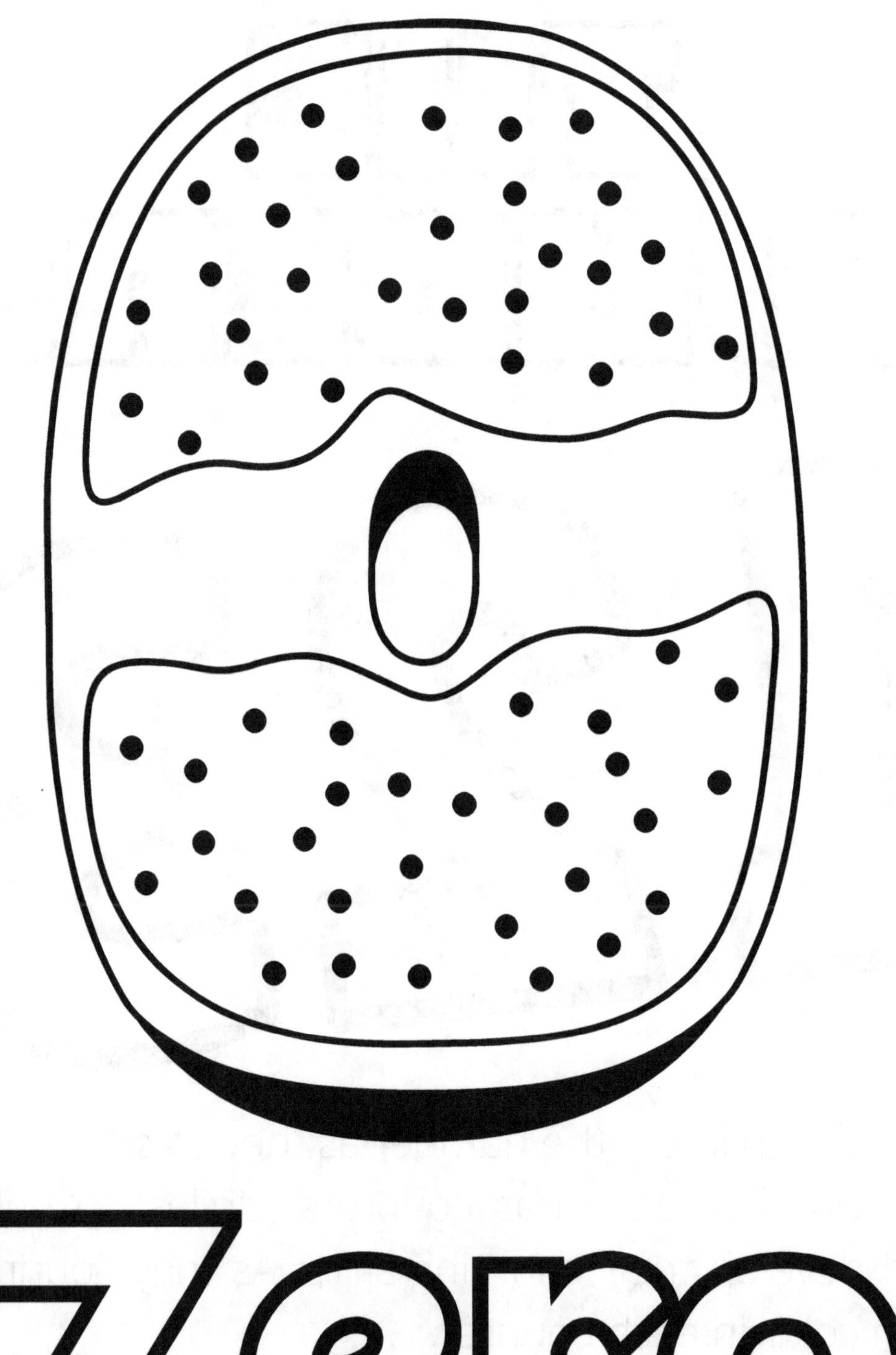

Zero

# One

TWO

Three

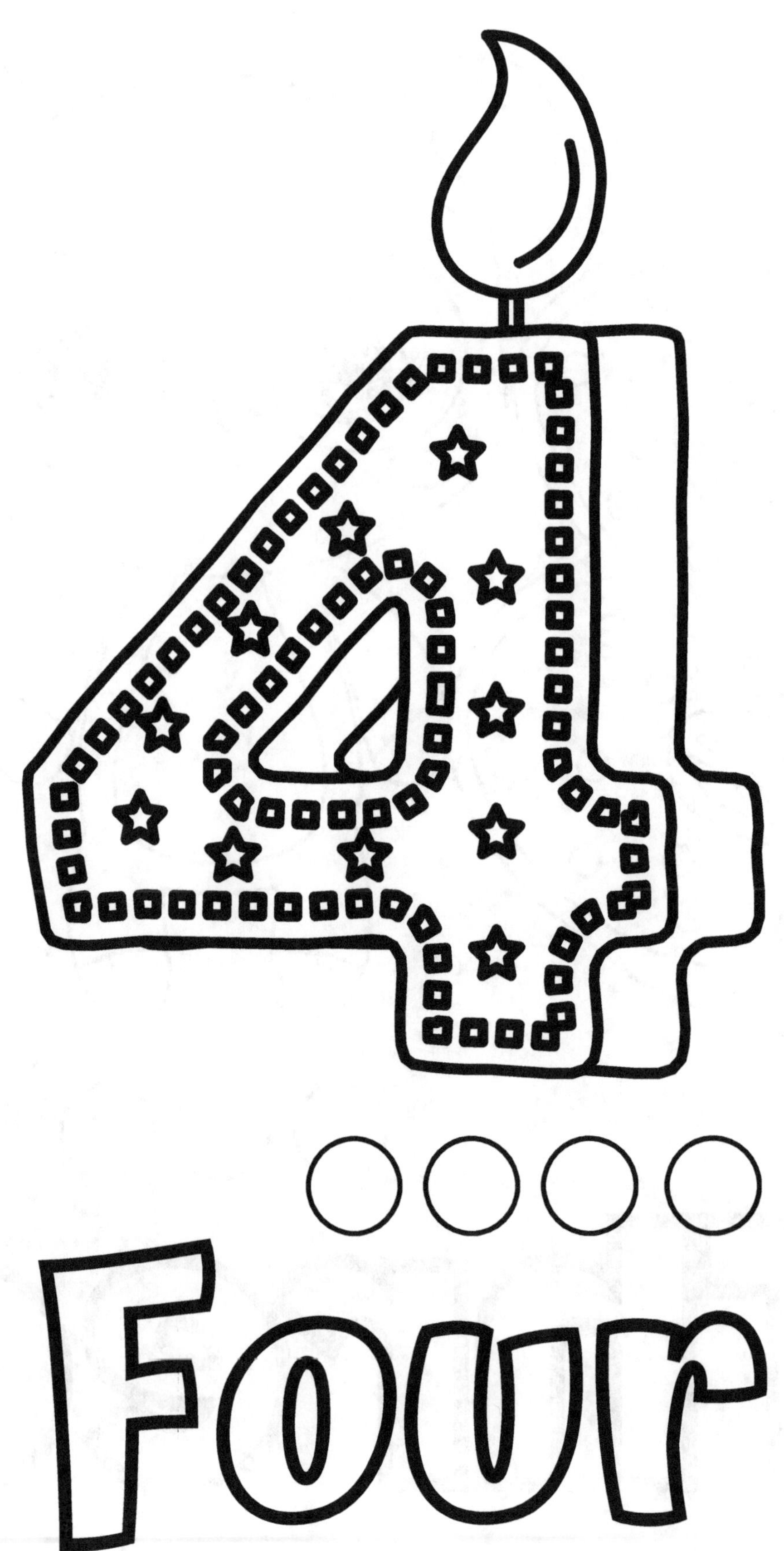

Four

# Five

Six

seven

# Eight

# Nine

Ten

# Eleven

# Twelve

Thirteen

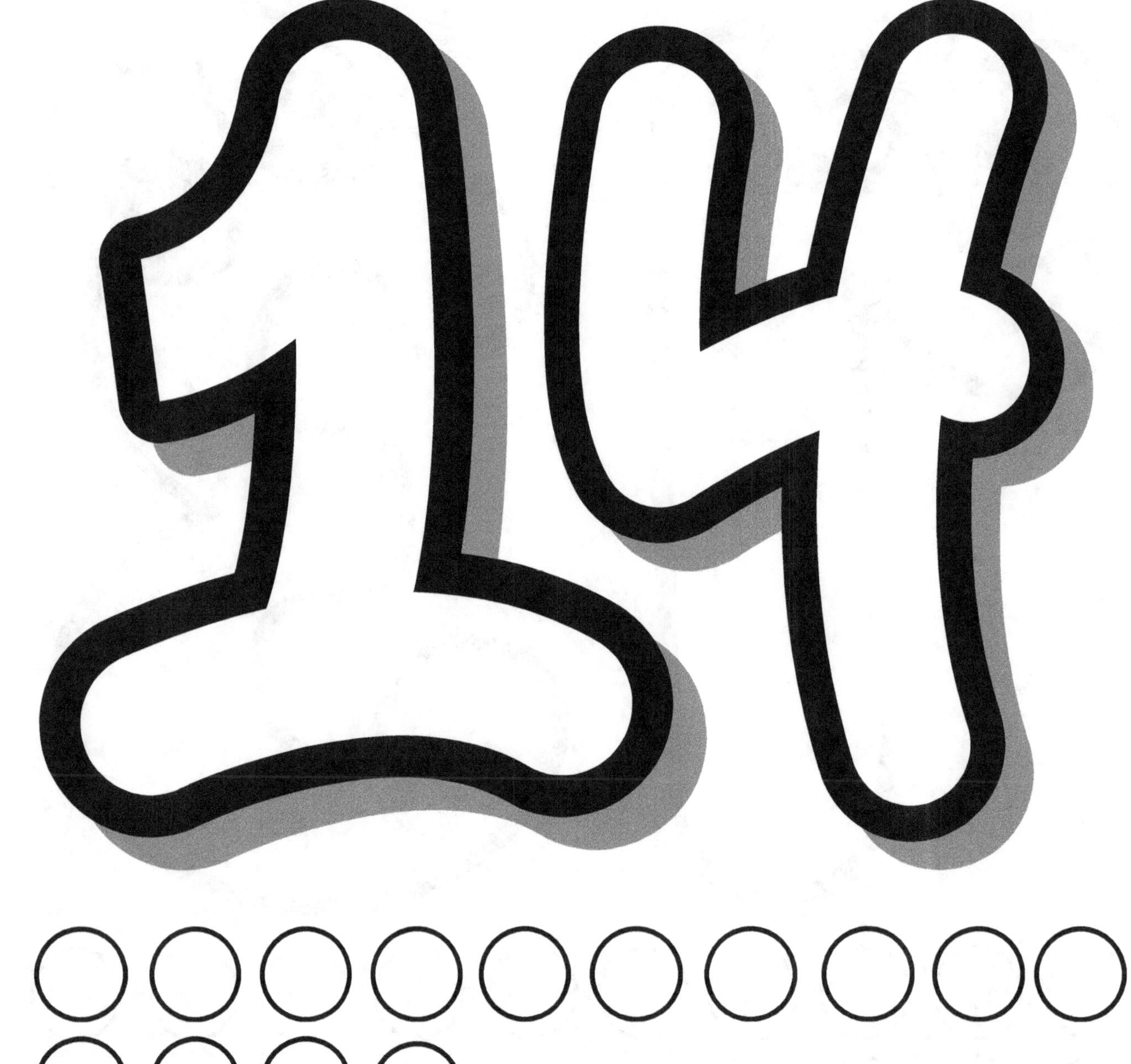

Fourteen

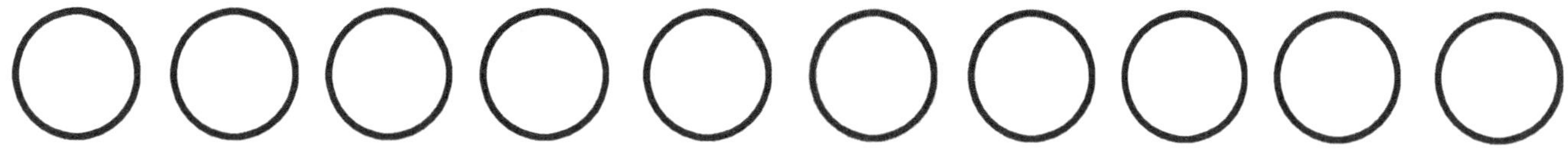

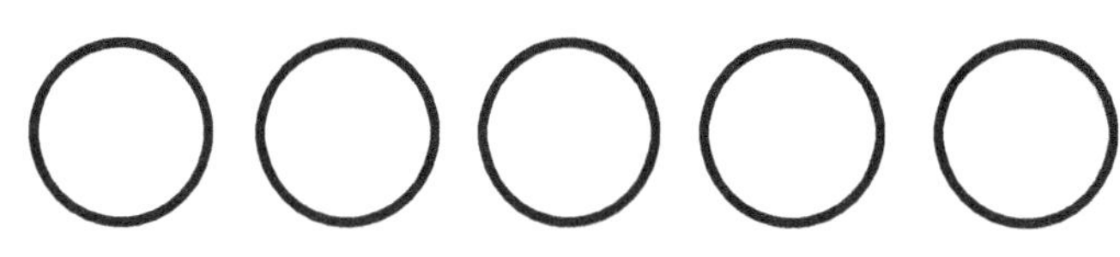

# Fifteen

sixteen

# Seventeen

# Eighteen

# Nineteen

Twenty

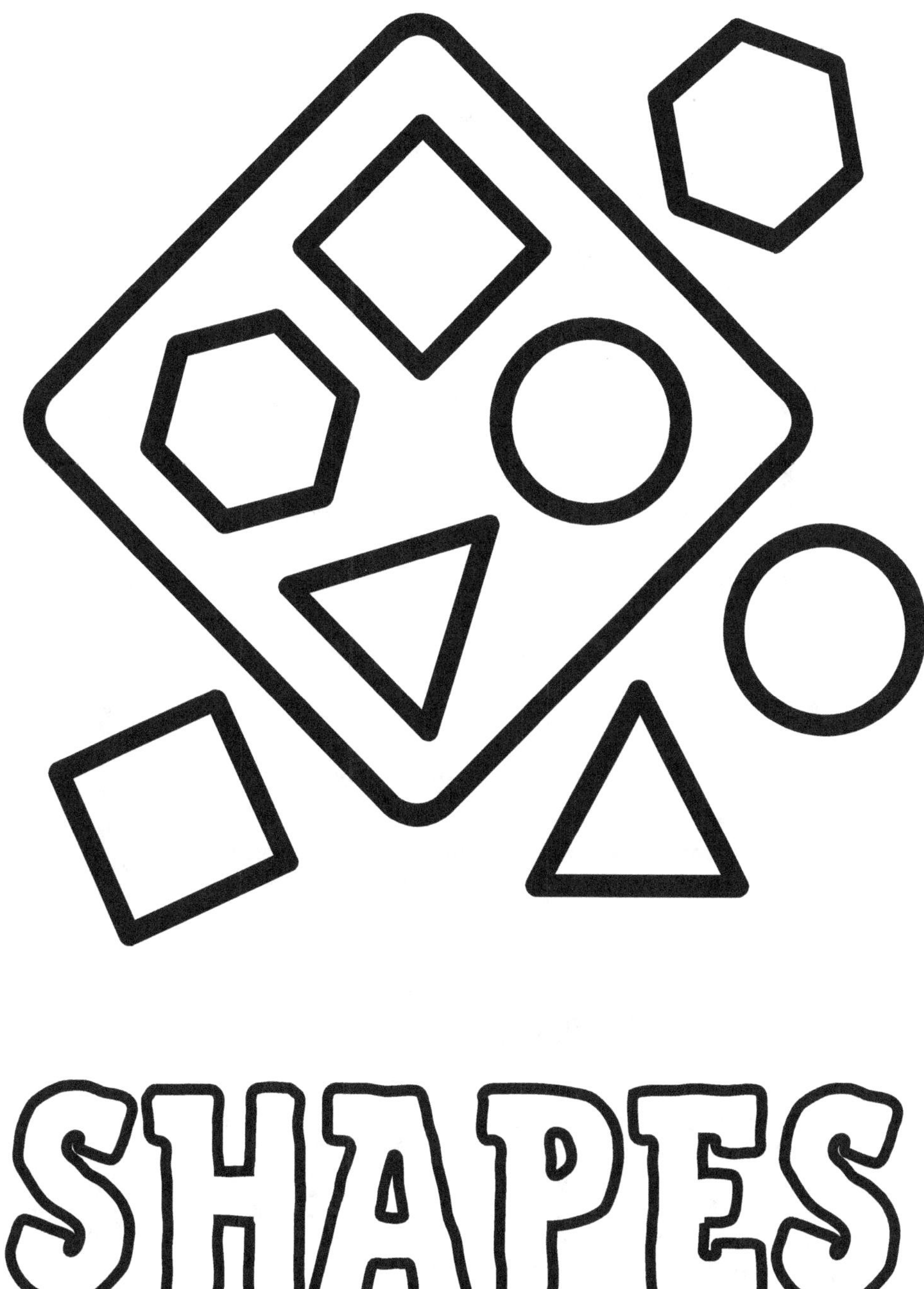

# SHAPES

# SQUARE

A slice of bread has the shape of a square.

# TRIANGLE

A slice of pizza has the shape of a triangle.

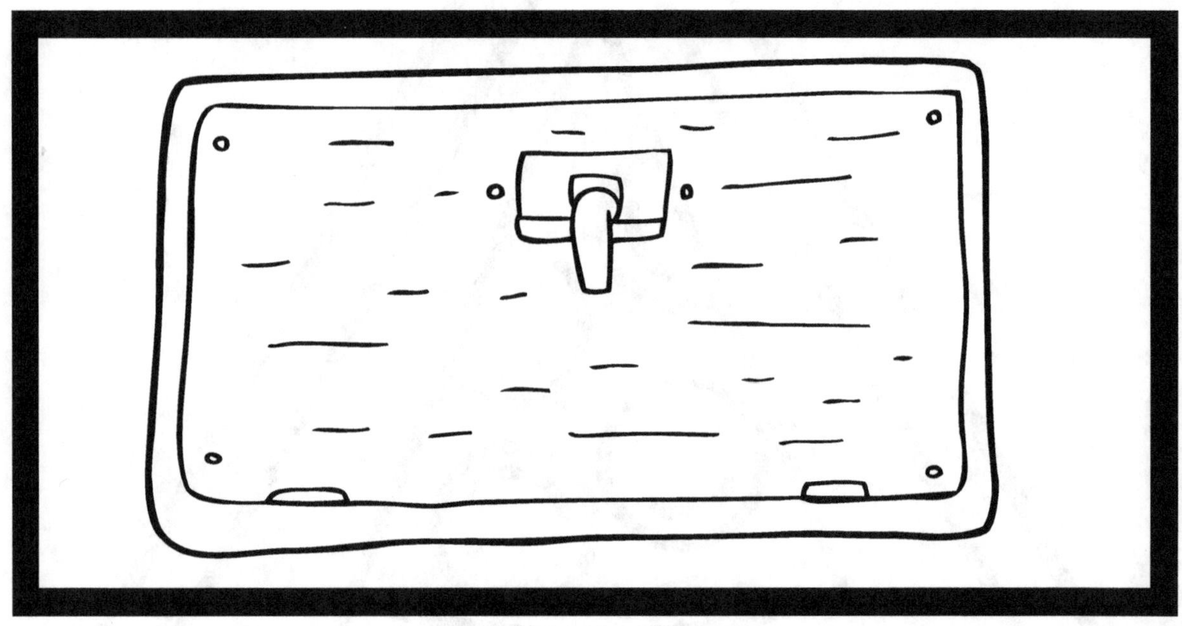

# RECTANGLE

The door has the shape of a rectangle.

# CIRCLE

The wheel has the shape of a circle.

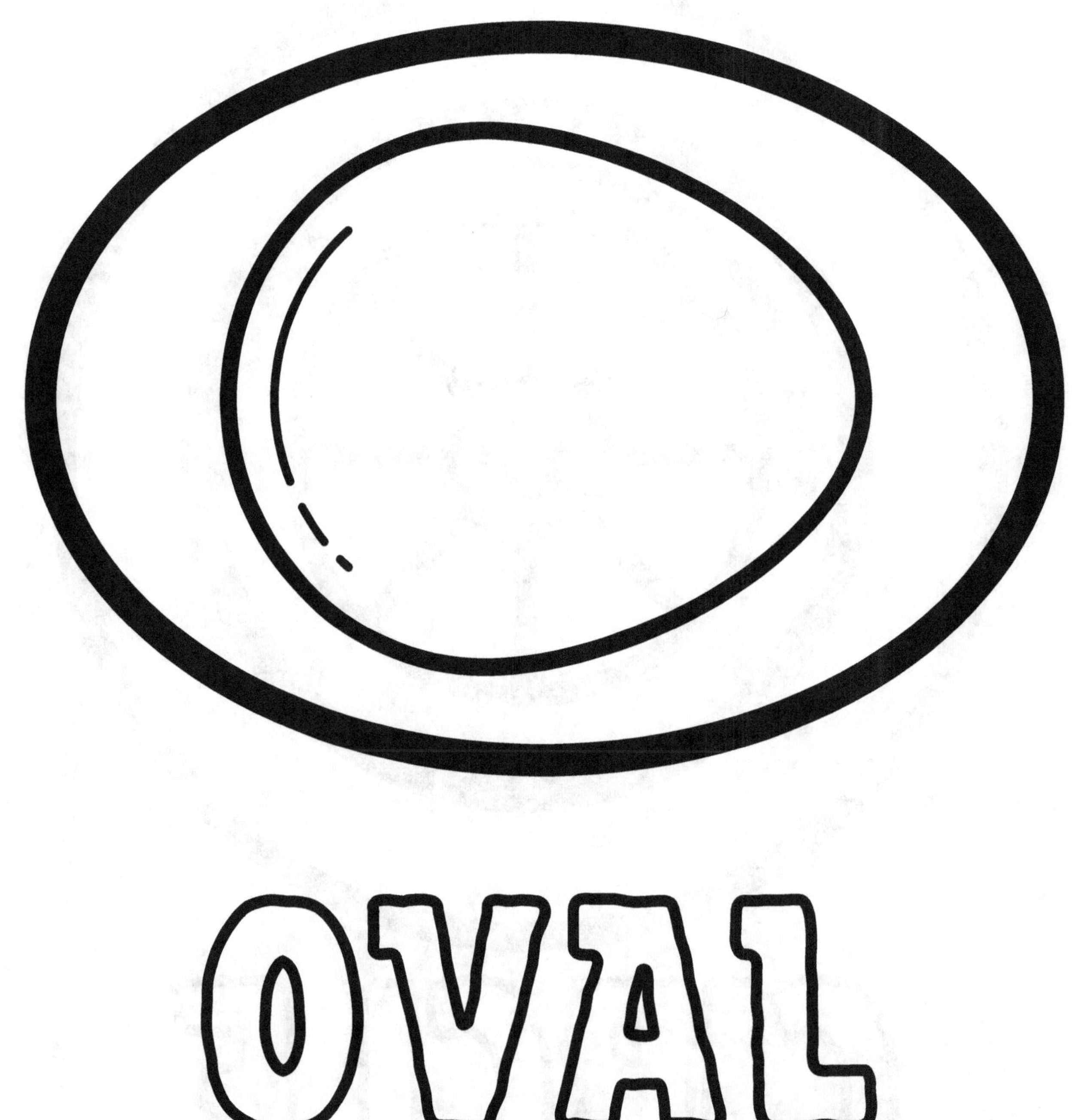

# OVAL

**The egg has the shape of an oval.**

**The starfish has the shape of a star.**

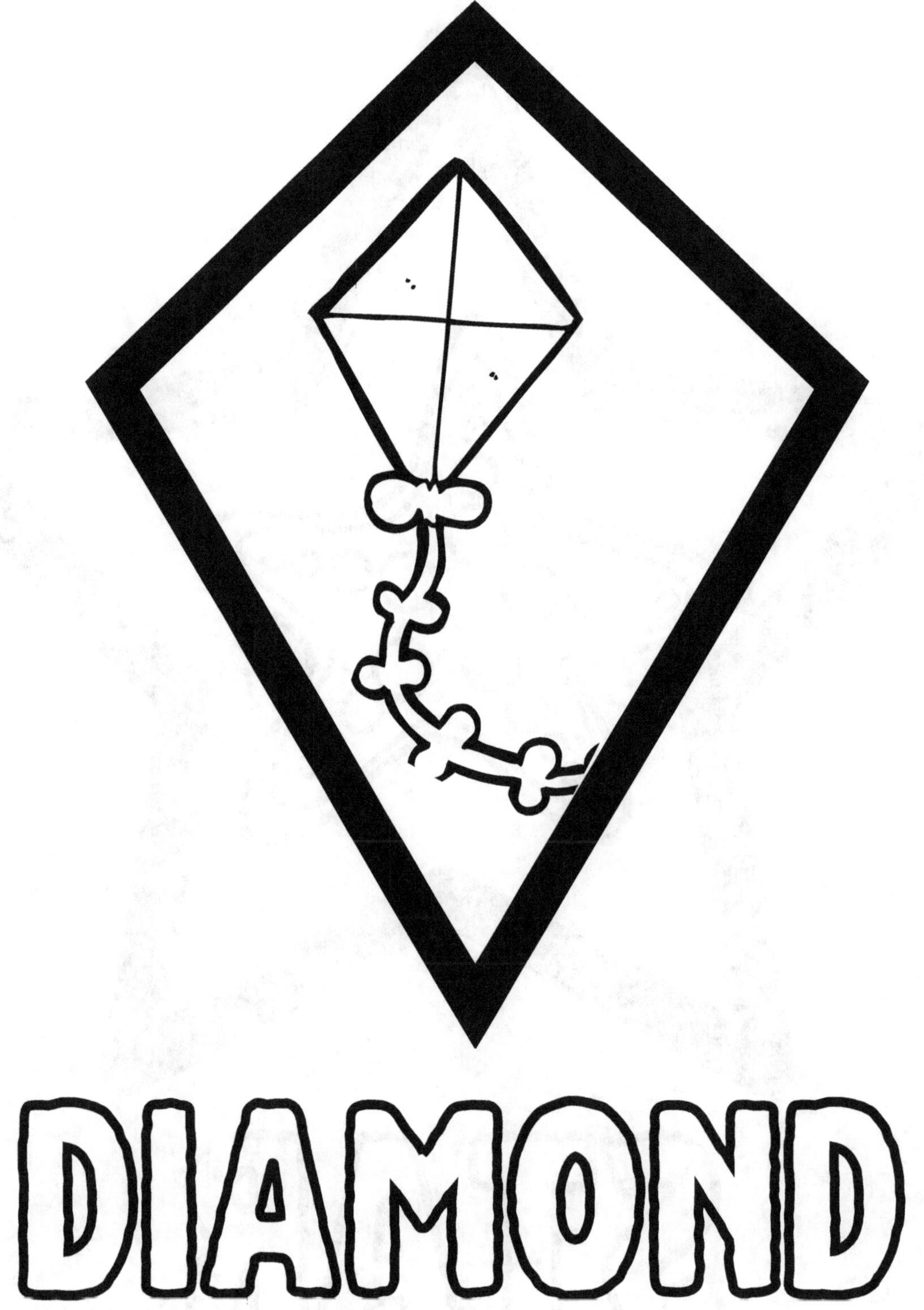

# DIAMOND

The kite has the shape of a diamond.

# HEART

The cherries have the shape of a heart.

# COLORS

# Yellow

**The babanas are yellow.**

# Red

**The apples are red.**

# Green

**The Trees are green.**

# Orange

**The oranges are orange.**

# Purple

**The grapes are purple.**

# Brown

**The football is brown.**

**The bunny is pink.**

# Gray

**The whale is gray.**

# Pink

**The bunny is pink.**

# Gray

**The whale is gray.**

**The bluebird is blue.**

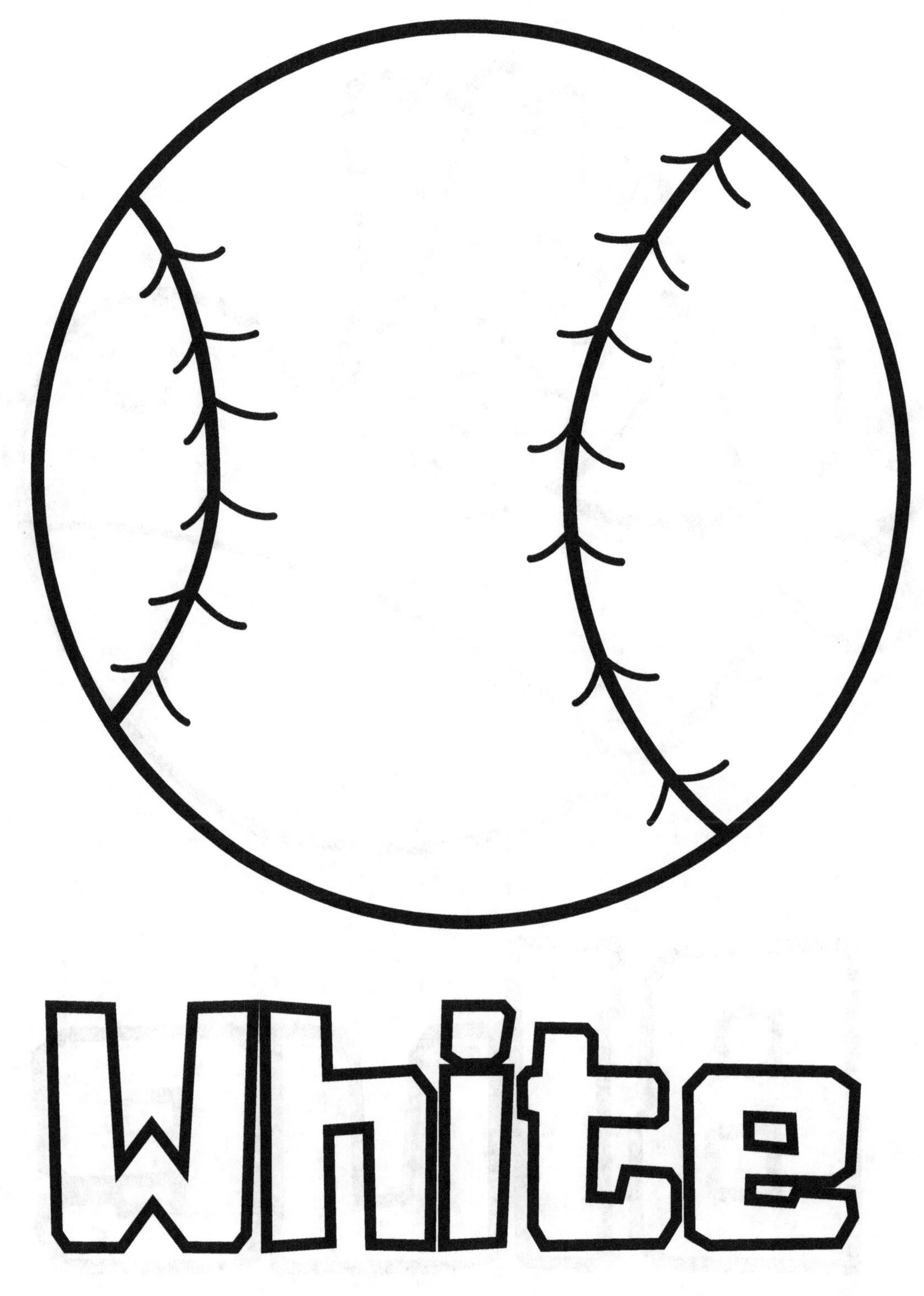

# White

**The baseball is white.**

# Black

**The dog is black.**

# COMMUNITY HELPERS

# TEACHER

POLICE

# FIREFIGHTER

# DOCTOR

# NURSE

# MAILMAN

# MECHANIC

# SOLDIER

DENTIST

# LAWYER

# TRANSPORTATION

CAR

BUS

# AIRPLANE

# TRUCK

TRAIN

BOAT

# MOTORCYCLE

# HELICOPTER

BICYCLE

ROCKETSHIP

# seasons

# WINTER

# SPRING

# SUMMER

# FALL

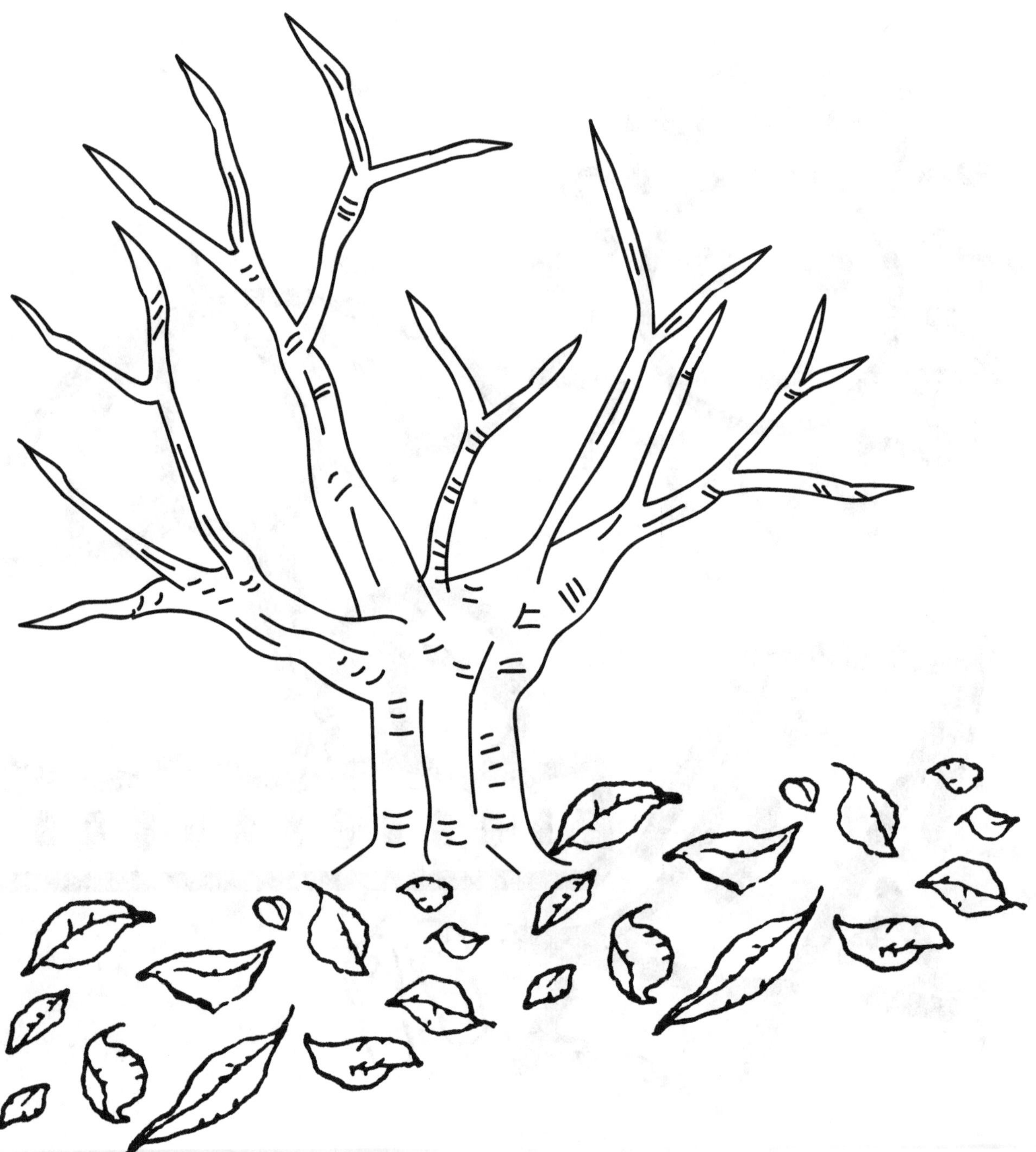

# We would love to hear from you, please review our book on Amazon. Thank you!

9 798583 221981